NOTHING TASTES QUITE LIKE A GERBIL

David Orme lives in Winchester and is the author of a wide range of poetry books, text books and picture books for children. When he is not writing he visits schools, performing poetry and running poetry workshops and encouraging children and teachers to enjoy poetry.

He likes gerbils but he has never eaten one.

Woody lives in London and has been illustrating children's books for the past eight years.

Also by Macmillan

'ERE WE GO!
Football Poems
chosen by David Orme

YOU'LL NEVER WALK ALONE
More Football Poems
chosen by David Orme

DRACULA'S AUNTIE RUTHLESS
and other Petrifying Poems
chosen by David Orme

SNOGGERS
Slap 'n' Tickle Poems
chosen by David Orme

THE SECRET LIVES OF TEACHERS
Revealing Rhymes
chosen by Brian Moses

NOTHING TASTES QUITE LIKE A GERBIL

and

other vile verses

chosen by
David Orme

and illustrated by
Woody

MACMILLAN CHILDREN'S BOOKS

First published 1996 by
Macmillan Children's Books
a division of Macmillan Publishers Ltd
25 Eccleston Place London SW1W 9NF
and Basingstoke

Associated companies throughout the world

ISBN 0 330 34632 6

1   3   5   7   9   8   6   4   2

A CIP catalogue record for this book is available from the British Library.

Typeset by Macmillan Children's Books
Printed by Mackays of Chatham plc, Kent

To the students and staff of
Corpus Christi School, Portsmouth

Contents

The Worm's Refusal

'This book's revolting!'
said the worm in a rage.
'I wouldn't be seen dead
on a single page.
I'm off. I'm leaving,
and that's that!
Wait . . . no!
don't slam it shut yet . . .
Aaaaaaargh!' SPLAT!

Tony Mitton

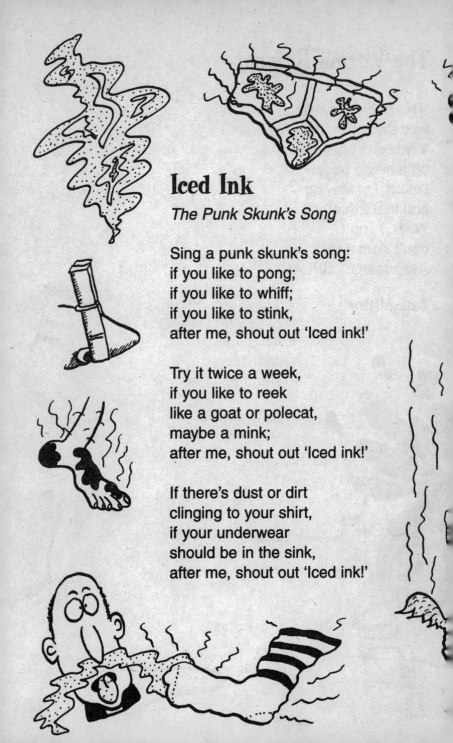

Iced Ink

The Punk Skunk's Song

Sing a punk skunk's song:
if you like to pong;
if you like to whiff;
if you like to stink,
after me, shout out 'Iced ink!'

Try it twice a week,
if you like to reek
like a goat or polecat,
maybe a mink;
after me, shout out 'Iced ink!'

If there's dust or dirt
clinging to your shirt,
if your underwear
should be in the sink,
after me, shout out 'Iced ink!'

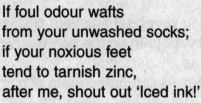

If you never clench
your nose at the stench,
when your nostril shocks
make the vicar blink,
after me, shout out 'Iced ink!'

If foul odour wafts
from your unwashed socks;
if your noxious feet
tend to tarnish zinc,
after me, shout out 'Iced ink!'

Sing a punk skunk's song:
if you like to pong;
if you like to whiff;
if you like to stink,
after me, shout out 'Iced ink!'

Mike Johnson

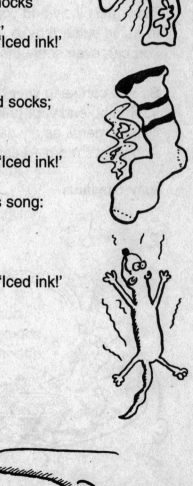

Nothing Tastes Quite Like a Gerbil

Nothing tastes quite like a gerbil
They're small and tasty to eat –
Morsels of sweet rodent protein
From whiskers to cute little feet!

You can bake them, roast them or fry them,
They grill nicely and you can have them *en croûte*,
In garlic butter they're simply delicious
You can even serve them with fruit.

So you can keep your beef and your chicken,
Your lamb and your ham on the bone,
I'll have gerbil as my daily diet
And what's more – I can breed them at home!

Tony Langham

Watch It!

It was the sort of day Miss Law liked best;
The pupils, in silence, doing a test.
The Secretary poked her head round the door,
'There's a telephone call for you Miss Law.'
Miss Law announced, 'Before I leave,
I've a trick for you lot up my sleeve.

I shall know precisely who's been working,
Who's been cheating, who's been shirking.'
Then she pulled a spoon from her trouser pocket
And levered her left eye out of its socket.
She plopped it into the goldfish bowl.
'So you know that I'll be watching y'all.'

She adjusted her hair and straightened her gown,
Left the eyeball in charge, bobbing up and down,
They wanted to scream, but no one dared
Before the eyeball's unblinking stare.
So they worked for a while under its scrutiny,
Heads down, silent, not a sign of mutiny,

Until a voice cried out – it was Christine Botching,
'I can't concentrate with that thing watching.
This eyeball prank leaves me disgusted
That Miss Law thinks we can't be trusted.'
She raced to the front, all flushed and pink
And tipped the eyeball down the sink.

Just at that moment the door swung wide.
Enter Miss Law, who in horror cried,
'You wicked girl. What have you done?
My eyeball gone. Now, I've only one.
Unless in my handbag, I have a spare.'
She looked. She wept. It wasn't there.

Outside, in the yard, Mr Payne,
The caretaker, was clearing the drain,
When he felt something round in his rubber-gloved
        paw.
The missing eyeball owned by Miss Law.
He tapped on the window, 'May I ask,
If this marble belongs to one of your class?'

'My eyeball,' cried Miss Law, clearly delighted.
'Mr Payne you truly deserve to be knighted.'
She rinsed her eyeball under the tap
Dried it out and pushed it back.
Then she looked at the class with a puzzled frown.
'I've put the thing in upside down.'

She gave her head a mighty clout
And into her hand the eye popped out.
Mr Payne gulped, 'What a horrible trick.
I've handled an eyeball. I'm going to be sick!'
Whilst the caretaker heaved over his drain
Miss Law slipped her eyeball back in again.

'That's better. Much more revealing.
I thought the class was on the ceiling.
Now, unless it's all my imagination,
This class was doing an examination.
So back to work. And children do
Remember, I've got my eye on you.'

John Coldwell

Grave Yard

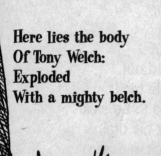

Here lies the body
Of Tony Welch:
Exploded
With a mighty belch.

Here lies the body
Of Mary Rose.
She ate the gunge
Between her toes.

Here lies the body
Of Tracey Plumb:
Sucked her body away –
– Began with her thumb!

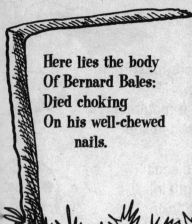

Here lies the body
Of Bernard Bales:
Died choking
On his well-chewed
nails.

Here lies the body
Of Auntie Betty:
Jogged thirty miles
Drowned – far too sweaty.

Here lies the body
Of young Len Loader,
Gassed to death
By his body odour.

John Kitching

Food for Thought

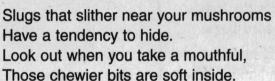

Slugs that slither near your mushrooms
Have a tendency to hide.
Look out when you take a mouthful,
Those chewier bits are soft inside.

Flies that settle on your biscuit
Stay so still and blend right in.
Look out for the bits that tickle
Just as you are swallowing.

Worms that wander near spaghetti
Lose their footing and fall in.
Look out, for that bit you're sucking
Looks as if it's wriggling.

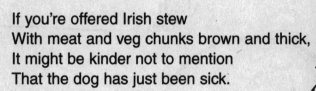

If you sneeze when near green chutney
Have the goodness to confess,
Suspicious lumps and slimy green bits
Could occasion some distress.

If you're offered Irish stew
With meat and veg chunks brown and thick,
It might be kinder not to mention
That the dog has just been sick.

Michaela Morgan

My Job Is:

to follow closely where you go,
to stretch in places where you grow,
to hold together blood and bones,
to fit round complicated zones,
to be a breeding ground for spots,
to pimple, sweat and smell because
to be around you is my lot –
to stick with you until we rot.

What am I?

Gina Douthwaite

Glunk

'What
Are you boiling in that pot?'

'Glunk.'

'Is that
Made from the tail
Of a plague-ridden rat,
The smear of a snail,
And the stink of a skunk,
Mixed in a mess of rotten plums
And severed thumbs?'

'No. That would be glook.
This is glunk – take a look.
Here's the recipe scribbled
Down in this bloodstained book: –
Glunk
Is rotten
And spotty
With spit and dribble,
Globules and gunge;
It's spongy
And grungy.
Watch how wasps plunge
Into it head first,
Then burst! Burst!! Burst!!!

If you stick the tip
Of your finger in glunk
Or have a sip,
You'll pass out – clunk
In the middle of the floor?'

'So what's glunk for?'

'It's a spell –
To catch
A struggling batch
Of green-nosed aliens in
A sardine tin or a rubbish bin.
With glunk our team will always win
Every football match.'

'Well,
I guess . . .
It doesn't work, but it sure is a mess,
And it makes a horrible smell.'

Leo Aylen

Hot Sizzling Lips

Chips.
Egg and chips.
Sausage, egg and chips.
Pork sausage, egg, baked beans and chips.
Pork sausage, fried leg, baked beans and chips.
Pork sausage, fried leg, baked beans and lips.
Pork sausage, fried legs, faked fiends, mushrooms
  and lips.
Cork sausage, fried legs, caked fiends, flushed
  foam and lips.
Cork garbage, fried legs, caked spleens, slushed
  foam, fried bread and lips.
Cork garbage, tied legs, caked spleens, crushed
  gnomes, tired Fred, bread and butter and lips.

Two cork garbages, two tied legs, caked spleens,
  crushed gnomes, tired Fred, bed and nutter,
  tomatoes and lips.

Glue cork garbages, blue tied legs, caked spleens,
  crushed gnomes, tired Fred, bed and nutter, torn
  toes, fresh green peas and lips.

Glue cork garbages, blue tied legs, caked spleens,
  crushed gnomes, tired Fred, bed and nutter, torn
  toes, flesh hardened flees and hot! sizzling! LIPS!

Paul Johnson

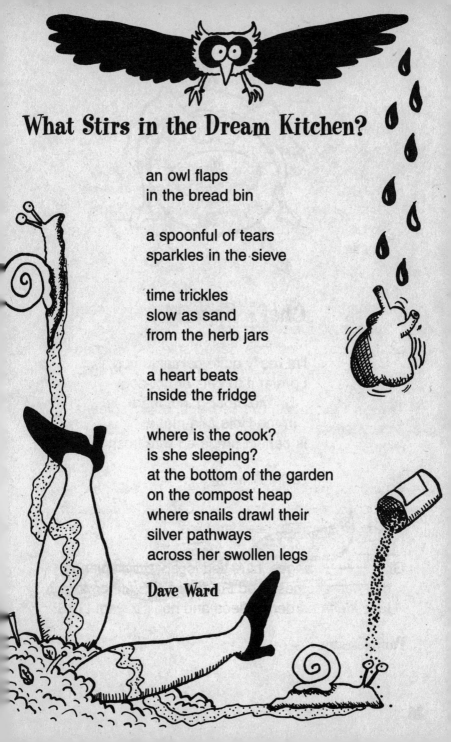

What Stirs in the Dream Kitchen?

an owl flaps
in the bread bin

a spoonful of tears
sparkles in the sieve

time trickles
slow as sand
from the herb jars

a heart beats
inside the fridge

where is the cook?
is she sleeping?
at the bottom of the garden
on the compost heap
where snails drawl their
silver pathways
across her swollen legs

Dave Ward

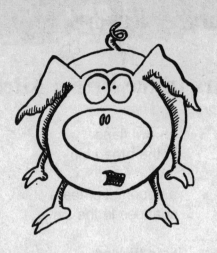

Chef's Special

I'm really quite partial to hog;
I prefer it to eels or hot-dog.
  On the other hand, toad-
  In-the-Hole à-la-mode
Is perfect prepared with fresh frog.

Cathy Benson

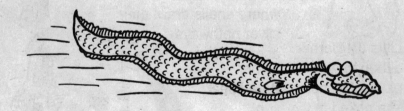

Nasty Nursery Rhymes

Little Miss Muffet
sat on a tuffet
eating old worms and hay
along came a spider
and sat down beside her –
she gobbled it up straight away.

Three biker mice
not very nice
see how they run
all mouth and gun
they crashed into a canal on Mars
and splintered their skulls on their handlebars
the ambulancemen scraped them into jars
three biker mice.

Old Mother Hubbard
went to the cupboard
to get her pet tiger some meat
but all she had got
was beans and carrots
so the tiger bit off both her feet.

Little Jill Horner
although we warned her
picked her nose with a spear;
she poked in too high,
snot shot from her eye
and brains dribbled out of her ear.

Dave Calder

Out at Lunch

All morning the rain had gobbed on the windows
and going over to lunch we all got soaked so that
you could hardly see the room for the steam rising
from wet clothes and wide tins of food and what
with the dank overpowering smells and the 'flu coming on
my head was swimming and as we're standing in this mist,
in line with our trays, JJ behind me says 'Look
worms in blood again' and though I knew he meant
the spaghetti I got this uneasy sensation
that the white mass was twitching but I felt so unsteady
I said nothing. It was like being inside a cloud,
not floating although my legs no longer felt sure
they were part of me and JJ's face seemed to swell
and his voice was at once far away and very loud
'Look cat stew, you can see bits of fur, cat spew stew,
look green sheep droppings, and is that maggots in rice
or rice in the maggots . . .' There was no stopping him
when he'd started this game, I tell you, one time he'd
put string in his curry and insisted it was a rat's tail
long after it was funny. 'Hey, I'd like some baked bugs please
with mashed brains and a giant slug.' My knees
were wobbly, I took a cheese roll and an orange juice
and even they seemed too much. When we sat down I felt worse,
I couldn't touch the food, I stared at the table, at the usual
crumbs, stains and slops, at JJ's plate opposite. Most
of all at his plate for it seemed like the beans

were squirming and one or two slid off, over the rim,
and scuttled away. It was a bit odd but I was past caring,
I felt like I was hanging over a huge pit, head spinning
so everything around was distant and dim
except for JJ's blether, now a meaningless babble
of surging waves through the blurring mist
and his left fist gripping a fork he'd just jabbed
into the mound of pale mashed potato
that looked strangely like I thought my brain felt inside my head
and when with a slow slither
the sausage twisted sideways and bit into his wrist
I fainted.

Dave Calder

Grandma's Dream

I think of Grandma telling her dream
that came back year after year, the same –

Like seeing the same old film, she said.
She'd be going along a country road,

The leaves were falling, and there were the gates
(horses' heads on the weather-worn posts),

In at the gates and down the drive
(with the yellow tower above the dark grove),

And down the drive and up to the door
by the shallow steps that braved the glare

Of rows of windows, blank as the water
in a dead canal by a summer shadow –

And over the threshold, and into the hall.
From the gilded ceiling the air hung still.

No one challenged her, no voice spoke,
no cough, no footstep, rustle or click.

Between two pillars of twisting marble,
framed like a stage stood a massive table

In all that splendour, she said, spread thick
from end to end with rubbish and muck –

There were screwed-up papers grey with grease,
furry bread crusts, slivers of glass,

Snot-glued tissues, hairs and skin,
curd-blotched bottles and a gristly bone . . .

Teabags, cans, rags . . . Grandma stared.
Far down the hall a shadow stirred.

A dark arched door began to open
for a girl with a tray, in a long apron.

The girl saw Grandma in her dream,
dropped the tray with a wild scream
and flung her apron up over her face –

She always woke at the same place.

Grandma's dream. Or Grandma a ghost
for a real girl somewhere, in a real house?

Libby Houston

What Class 4 Wish the Most

We wish our teacher
would not push
his pencil in his ear.

Not the sharp bit
but the blunt bit
it's the moment we all fear.

He wriggles it
he jiggles it
turns it round and round.

Then pulls it out
with a squidgy slurp
looks at what he's found.

Sometimes it's runny
like golden honey
dripping on his tie.

Or brown as coffee
like sticky toffee
crusty as a pie.

First he sniffs it
then he licks it
wipes it on his sleeve.

Then uses it
to mark our sums
makes our stomachs heave.

David Harmer

The Scumbags' Song

As performed by Earwig, Molar, Piggy, Scab,
Spots, Dustbin, Lavvy, and Scum

Ohhhhhhhhh
we love diggin' in dustbins
we love scratchin' our toesies
we love eatin' spiders
and we love pickin' our noses.
Hey hey
hey hey hey
hey hey hey hey hey
HEY!

Ohhhhhhhhh
we love dancin' in discos
we love rippin' our trousies,
we love pinchin' bottoms
and we wear frilly girls' blouses
Hey hey
hey hey hey
hey hey hey hey hey
HEY!

Ohhhhhhhhh
we love rockin' 'n' rollin'
we love makin' loud noises
we love shoutin' 'YER WOT?'
Yeah, we're the scummiest boysies.
Hey hey
hey hey hey
hey hey hey hey hey
HEY!

Wes Magee

Blow This

Who
knows
why   a
nose   has
hair?   Don't
despair   for
it's   there
to   deter
the   entry   of
dust   which
turns   to   a crust,
clogs   nostrils
and   blocks   off
t   h   e   a   i   r

Gina Douthwaite

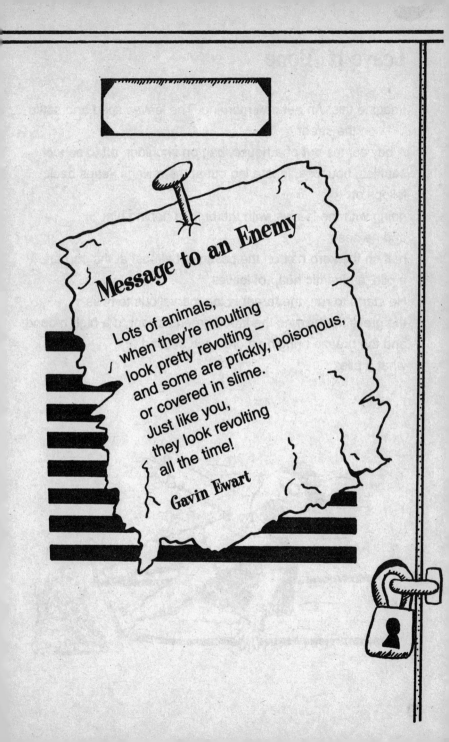

Message to an Enemy

Lots of animals,
when they're moulting
look pretty revolting –
and some are prickly, poisonous,
or covered in slime.
Just like you,
they look revolting
all the time!

Gavin Ewart

Leave it Alone

Imagine this. An autumn morning. The leaves scud and settle
   on the street
A boy comes out of a house, bag on shoulder, off to school,
shuffles, bounces, jabs a leg out at the railings, leaps back,
lollops on
going with the leaves, with the breeze behind him
and he sees
half on the kerb half on the pavement almost at the corner
a pile, a gigantic heap of leaves.
He starts to run, the target is too marvellous to miss,
the greys the browns the faded greens swept to a high mound,
and the breeze bringing more each second
what a pile.

And his legs ready themselves for that good kick
that ploughing explosive rush through crackling dryness
and he comes to the moment,
hold it
imagine it, that moment
the moment all warriors, drivers, rulers fear
and a thought goes down to the pit of his stomach
a message drops to the bottom of his boots
that he knows something's terribly wrong but can't spot it
and he's going too fast, he can't stop
hold it, that moment, that important moment
before he hits
and slips and skids
on the brown steaming curd buried under the leaves
as his clothes, his face are plastered in a thick crusty mass
and coated with leaves at interesting angles
and when he stands up – what to do, to go home, to stand
in the shower in his clothes – to strip off there and then
before the smell does for him? and as he hovers in despair
he wipes his face with the cleaner side of a sleeve
shuffles to the corner and there,
still not far down the street
is the elephant.

Dave Calder

How to Scare Your Gran
(but not Mine!)

First get green putty
cover one eye
distort the nose
roll out wafers of green skin
to pat smoothly on up to the hairline

Take half a ping pong ball
paint on a staring bloodshot eye
and stick it halfway down the cheek

Squelch out a handful of green gel
rub it over the hair
pull up into spikes

Stuff a fat cushion
up the back of your jumper

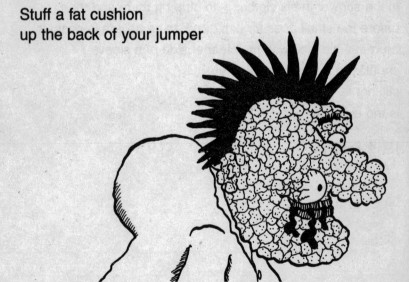

Tie a dressing gown
round your shoulders

Turn on the lamps
with the purple bulbs

Put the foaming blood capsule
ready between your lips

Stand behind the door and wait
for gran to arrive

Her keys are jangling
she's opening the door
I'm leaping out
YAAAAAAAAAAAAAAARRRRRRRRGH!

'Hello our Kevin.
I've brought you some chips
My word, you look more like
your grandad every day.'

Rita Ray

Down with Flu!

I've a bag code,
fluey and flemmy
in me node;

feel like somebobby's
stuffed
a hod wed towel
insibe
me achin' heb;

I've a scratchy frob
in me throde,
me chest's full
ob frobspawn;

I wheeze and explose
ashoo-ashoo-ashoo
into me hankersneeze,
I tishoo-tishoo-tishoo
into me tishoo;

I've a bag code
in me node,
and I'm feb up,
really feb up,

really, really, really
feb up here in beb.

Matt Simpson

Feeling Down in the Mouth

Our teacher took his false teeth off the shelf
But put them in the wrong way round –
The outcome was that he slowly ate himself
Until the only trace of him that could be found;
Were his false teeth, grinning on the playground.

David R. Morgan

Dear Gran

When I sit on your knee, Gran,
I can see right up your nose.
You must be really old, Gran,
To grow hairs as long as those.

You must be really old, Gran,
To have wrinkles on your chin.
Isn't it hard to tell, Gran,
Where your chin and neck begin?

One tooth is wobbly – look, Gran!
So, before I'm eighty-two,
Will I take all MY teeth out –
Like you and Grandad do?

I love you very much, Gran,
As everyone can see –
And not JUST because of the sweets, Gran,
That I HOPE you've brought for me . . .

Trevor Harvey

Licking Toads

'What I want to know is this,'
said Sharon. 'Is kissing Barry Reynolds
worse than licking toads,
or do they rate about the same
on any top ten list of hates?'
So we did a survey, round
all the girls in our year.
'Would you rather the toad or Barry?'
And everyone had to answer
or Sharon threatened to twist
their arms, but Melissa said
it was cruel to go on about Barry,
and we poked fun and said,
'You going to marry him are you?'
And then, when we counted
the votes, it seemed most girls
preferred to chance the toad
than risk kissing Barry.
Sharon said, 'You'd catch less
from the toad.' And then we said
'Let's try again, would you rather
eat a tarantula egg omelette?'
But no one was quite
so sure about that!

Brian Moses

Excuse me, is this your Skull?

My mother said
I should get ahead –
But I don't think this one's mine;
I've just found it in the potting shed
By the 'Deadly Nightshade' sign . . .

Trevor Harvey

Grime and Punishment

When I've got ice-cream up my nose,
mud between my toes
and plasticine under every nail;
my shirt is ripped,
my zip's unzipped
and the jam sandwich in my pocket's gone stale;
there's gunge in my hair,
a funny stain down there,
I know what's going to happen without fail:
my dad won't stop to laugh,
I'll be dunked in the bath,
then he'll point to my bedroom and say JAIL.

Stephen Clarke

The Cake that Makes you Scream

Underneath the icing,
Underneath the cream,
Underneath the marzipan
Is the cake that makes you scream.

It's filled with sticky spiders,
Slugs and earwigs too,
And swarms of tiny beetles
Swimming round in glue.

Underneath the icing,
Underneath the cream,
Underneath the marzipan
Is the cake that makes you scream.

It's filled with vampires' fingernails
And all their fingers too,
Crawling from the oozing sludge
Just to tickle you.

Underneath the icing,
Underneath the cream,
Underneath the marzipan
Is the cake that makes you scream.

It's filled with twisted nightmares
Where strawberries turn blue,
And fishes' legs and donkey eggs
Growl and howl and moo.

Underneath the icing,
Underneath the cream,
Underneath the marzipan
Is the cake that makes you scream.

When you cut this curious cake
You don't know what you'll find;
Be careful or the slimy jam
Will climb inside your mind.

But even more important,
Be careful with the knife:
It'll try and slice your tongue out
Before you can take a bite.

Then you won't taste the icing,
And you won't taste the cream,
And the marzipan will slobber out
In a sickening, shapeless scream.

Dave Ward

How to make a Mummy

1. Take one dead body, *not necessarily Egyptian*,
   and wash it with wine and spices.

   That's the good bit, because

2. Shove a long hook up its nose and drag out the
   brains.

   And

3. Cut open its belly, take out the guts, the lungs and
   any other lumps of gunge that you can find, before
   stuffing the whole thing with a kind of salt that
   will soak up the wet.

   BUT

   you *must* leave the body on a slope so that
   you can catch any juice that runs out.

4. After about forty days, the body (or what's left
   of it) should be dry. Now you have to wash it,
   outside and inside, with oil and smellies.

   Being shrivelled up, like a human prune, and
   somewhat empty inside, the stiff won't look quite
   himself, so

5. Stuff the head and body with linen soaked in sweet-smelling oil, so that it might look like a bit like it did when you first started.

6. Decorate and wrap.

P.S. This isn't really a poem. I just thought you might be interested.

Mike Jubb

Snot-Rags

One day when Mr and Mrs Mucus
were busy wiping Dewdrops
cousin Phlegm called –

'Snot-Rags, the local laundry,
are having a fete' he coughed.
'Lady Kleenex will be presenting
the 'Green Sleeves' award for
The Best Kept Nose.
Runners up will each receive
a fistful of used tissues.

There will be many other slime-shows.
Nosebola
Name the Nose
A knitted Nose-Cosy competition
Blow your own Bugle
The BIGGEST Beak
The Most Hideous Hooter
Guess the Weight of the Trunk
Sniff the Whiff
The Loudest Sneeze
and – Splat the Conk –
with a prize for the most bloodied nose –

and – for the first time ever,
this year, in the tea tent –
a delicious treat –
Pick Your Own Bogeys –
good enough to . . .'

Denise Bennett

Slowly Squeezing Squelchy Spots

Slowly squeeze
slowly squash
slowly squirt squashy spots
slowly shoot
slowly spurt
slowly staining shirts
shiny slimy stains
slippy sloppy stains
slippy slicky stains
slishy sloshy stains
slithering sliding seeping slowly
slowly squeezing slowly squashing
slowly squirming slowly sloshing
spurting shoots
shooting spurts
squirting shots
shooting squirts
slowly squeezing silly stupid squishy squashy spots
slowly squeezing silly stupid squishy squashy spots
Splat splash squelch!
Splat splash squelch!
Splat splash squelch splat squelch!

Paul Cookson

Growth or Moan

'She who stands in cow pat grows'
is how the age-old saying goes

so being tiny, too petite,
I slipped the shoes from off my feet
and shed the socks that warmed my toes
then poised in ballerina pose
to . . .
overbalance!
with a thrust
one foot broke through the cow pat crust
and pure manure of mustard hue
adorned where once I'd worn a shoe
whilst waves of warmth swept ankle high
and splattered splots festooned my eye

and even if I'd be believed
I can't tell what my mouth received
because that orifice is blocked
(with powers of speech severely shocked).

That age-old saying should, methinks,
be, '*She who stands in cow pat stinks.*'

Gina Douthwaite

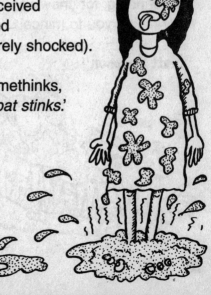

The Jaws that Snap

O keep me from the crocodile,
its knobbly thrashing rudder,
its beady greedy swivel eyes
that always make you shudder.

Keep me from the crocodile,
its wicked warty skin,
teeth as sharp as arrow heads,
its terrifying grin.

O save me from the crocodile,
the hinges of its jaws
which clap together chunk-chunk-chunk!
I know what they're for!

For biting, for chomping!
(don't they make you wince?)
for grinding, for chewing,
shredding you to mince!

Matt Simpson

Snoggers

Slap 'n' tickle poems chosen by David Orme

A great collection of poems
for Snoggers, Sniggerers,
Slappers and Ticklers.

Snogging

They were snogging in the High Street.
They were snogging in the yard.
They were snogging in the classroom.
They were snogging really hard.

They were snogging at the bus-stop
and in the canteen too.
They were snogging in the supermarket
standing in the queue.

They were snogging most of yesterday
and all the day before.
They were snogging in the changing room
just behind the door.

They were snogging on the playing field,
though it was lousy weather.
They snog so much, I think their lips
are superglued together.

Charles Thomson

Custard Pie

Poems that are jokes that are poems
Chosen by Pie Corbett

Love Poem

Her eyes were bright
as she reached out
and touched me with her
smooth, white hand.

I trembled,
excitedly;
as she happened
to be clutching
a live electric cable,
at the time.

Harry Munn

The Secret Lives of Teachers

Revealing rhymes about what teachers do in their spare time
Poems chosen by Brian Moses

What Teachers Wear In Bed!

It's anybody's guess
what teachers wear in bed at night
so we held a competition
to see if any of us were right.

We did a spot of research,
although some of them wouldn't say,
but it's probably something funny
as they look pretty strange by day.

Our Headteacher's quite old-fashioned,
he wears a Victorian nightshirt,
our sports teacher wears her tracksuit
and sometimes her netball skirt.

We asked our secretary what she wore
but she shooed us out of her room,
and our teacher said, her favourite nightie
and a splash of expensive perfume.

And Mademoiselle, who teaches French,
is really very rude,
she whispered, '*Alors*! Don't tell a soul,
but I sleep in the . . . back bedroom!'

Brian Moses

Sandwich Poets

The greatest hits of three poets in one tasty volume

Rice Pie & Moses

by John Rice, Pie Corbett and Brian Moses

and

Matt Wes & Pete

by Matt Simpson, Wes Magee and Peter Dixon